WORLD WAR I
SONGS & TUNES
for the
UKULELE

by Dick Sheridan

ISBN 978-1-57424-304-8
SAN 683-8022

Cover by James Creative Group

CENTERSTREAM®

Table of Contents

Introduction 5

About the Author 7

Songs (in alphabetical order)

Avalon.. 86

Back In The U.S.A. 96

Break The News To Mother 22

Caissons Go Rolling Along, The 84

Dardanella... 64

Don't Cry Frenchy 60

Down In The U-17 78

Fighting Sixty-Ninth, The 75

Garryowen 16

God Save The King...................................... 92

Good-Bye, Dolly Gray 23

Goodbye Broadway, Hello France.............. 52

Good Night, Germany 88

Hail! Hail! The Gang's All Here!................ 50

Hello Central, Give Me No Man's Land.................. 66

How 'Ya Gonna Keep 'Em Down On The Farm....... 17

Hunting The Hun 82

I Didn't Raise My Boy To Be A Soldier 10

I Wonder Who's Kissing Her Now.............. 26

I'm Always Chasing Rainbows 20

If I'm Not At The Roll Call......................... 28

If You Were The Only Girl In The World 12

It's A Long Way To Tipperary...................... 94

I've Got My Captain Working For Me 42

K-K-K-Katy 32

La Marseillaise 62

Mademoiselle From Armentières 54

My Melancholy Baby 38

Neutral is My Middle Name 14

Oh! Frenchy 55

Oh! How I Hate To Get Up In The Morning............. 46

Oh! Johnny Oh! 36

Oui! Oui! Marie 58

Over There 69

Rose Of No Man's Land, The 72

Rule Britannia 92

Silent Night.. 90

Smiles... 48

Taps.. 102

There's A Long, Long Trail.......................... 68

There's A Service Flag Flying At Our House........... 100

Till We Meet Again 30

We're In The Army Now 8

Where Do We Go From Here....................... 40

World Is Waiting For The Sunrise, The....... 74

Would You Rather Be A Colonel With An Eagle On Your Shoulder 44

Yankee Boy... 33

You're A Grand Old Flag............................. 98

An Introduction

From the muddy, bloody trenches of France and northern Europe – from the music halls of London to the footlights of Broadway and the din of Tin Pan Alley – from farms and cities and homelands across America – these are the songs of World War I. Songs of the Great War, the war supposedly to end all wars.

Over the span of five years, from 1914 to 1918, the world was in chaos. Germany was on the march with her allies of the Central Powers: Austria-Hungary, the Ottoman Empire, and initially Bulgaria. When American Expeditionary Forces under Gen. "Black Jack" Pershing landed in France in 1917, war had already been raging in France, Belgium, Russia, Greece, and Serbia. Of the two million American troops sent to France, one million would actually see combat, and over 50,000 of them would lose their lives.

The war was fought on land, sea and air. German zeppelins bombed London. American volunteers in France formed the famous flying group the Lafayette Escadrille. German submarines, at various times in unrestricted warfare, sought out passenger vessels, merchant ships, and convoys. Flying a British flag, the Lusitania with over 100 American lives was sunk by a German U-boat as the ship entered the Irish Channel. Sea battles, like that of Jutland, were fought by the British and Germans off the northern coast of England and the North Sea.

But it was the land battles on the Western and Eastern Fronts that produced the worst carnage and tribulations. Campaigns were fought from trenches with opposing sides separated only by shell holes and barbed wire. Dug to a depth of about six feet, the trenches filled with water and mud, rats and lice. At the command of "Up and over!" charges were mounted from step ladders. Poison gas that smelled like mustard drifted with the wind. Feet that were constantly soaked produced a painful condition known as "trench foot." Lightweight raincoats for officers replaced heavy rubber ones that gave rise to the name "trench coat." Surprisingly more lives were lost from illness than from actual combat.

There were the oddities of war. French troops rode to the front in taxi cabs. Armored tanks were secretly concealed in crates marked "water tanks," hence the vehicle's name. At the start of the war German helmets were made from boiled leather with a spike on top but later changed to the all-steel variety so familiar from World War II. Unofficial truces were sometimes declared at Christmas and New Year's with socialization between troops from both sides. German fighter pilot ace, Baron Manfred von Richthofen, who was credited with 80 kills, had his aircraft painted red, which earned him the nickname of "The Red Baron." Until metal became scare in Germany, Richthofen had each victory recorded on individual silver cups engraved with the date and type of aircraft downed.

War is always accompanied by music, and the Great War was no exception. There were old tunes and new ones; it is estimated that over 800 songs were written during the war and the years that came immediately after. The following collection is a representative sampling of this enormous output. There are songs of patriotism, propaganda, and those that boosted morale, promoted recruiting, and encouraged the sale of war bonds. Sentimental songs depicted the sad partings of young soldiers from their homes, sweethearts, and worried mothers. Boastful jingoistic songs reflected strong anti-German feelings. Comic songs eased the tension and added a bit of fun to the seriousness. Lively brass bands played spirited marches for parades and wharf-side send-offs as troops boarded ships for an uncertain crossing in U-boat infested waters. But not all songs were upbeat and optimistic. As the romance and reality of war turned to disillusionment, anti-war sentiment spread with resentment for America's breaking with neutrality and President Wilson's unfulfilled campaign promise of "He kept us out of war."

A counterbalance to military music was the outpouring of popular songs from Tin Pan Alley. Many of the songs written during this period and before were played and sung side by side with their war-related counterparts. Several of these songs are included here along with a brief list of other well-known numbers.

These were the years when popularity of the ukulele first took hold and started a craze that lasted for twenty years and is even now experiencing renewed interest. With its capability of beautiful tone and chordal harmony, the humble uke can capture every nuance and demand of these WWI songs. It's amazing how this small instrument with its four short strings and scaled-down fretboard can perfectly handle such range and subtleties. But it can, and does so with surprising effect that recreates so vividly a unique time gone by.

It's all here waiting for you, melodic tunes and lyrics rich in imagery. Drift back in time to a hundred years ago, bring the past to the present, and discover how immortal this music can be. From the shadows of a bygone time "there's a long, long, trail a-winding" and it reaches to us now in the memorable pages to follow.

The Salvation Army band. Founded in 1865 in London by Methodist minster William Booth to bring salvation to the poor, destitute and hungry. The women helped at the front running canteens, making apple pies for the boys and creating a little touch of home.

About The Author

World War I was before Dick Sheridan's time, but he was a youngster during the Second World War, and his memories of those days are still very much with him.   He recalls air raid sirens, nighttime black-outs, and helmeted wardens patrolling the darkened streets. He remembers how empty lots were converted into Victory Gardens, how gasoline was rationed as were cigarettes and many food items including coffee, sugar, and meat. Military uniforms were a common sight, and every branch of service was represented. People bundled cardboard and newspapers for the war effort, put them out for special trash pickups along with kitchen fat that could be converted into munitions. Kids likewise contributed scraps of tin foil they had rolled up into giant balls. At school, Liberty Stamps could be purchased for a quarter and placed in a special booklet. When enough stamps were assembled the booklet could be converted into a War Bond.

As did many kids, Dick collected military items – colorful unit badges and patches along with arm and shoulder insignia that denoted both enlisted and officer ranks. Model airplanes hung from the ceiling of his bedroom with P-38s and Grumman Hellcats doing aerial battle with Japanese Zeros and German Messerschmitts. Not to be forgotten was the memory of his father tensely hearing the news on the radio that the Japanese had bombed Pearl Harbor and President Roosevelt's announcement that war was declared.

Over the airwaves came songs like "Johnny Got A Zero," "Coming In On A Wing And A Prayer," and British vocalist Vera Lynn singing "The White Cliffs of Dover" and "We'll Meet Again." The Andrew Sisters sang about the boogie woogie bugle boy from Company B.   Everyone was singing, "You can keep your shaving cream and lotion, if I'm going to cross the ocean, give me a girl in my arms tonight …"

Although this was World War II, parallels can easily be drawn with the "war to end all wars" which preceded it. Not that World War I was really that far away: Dick had an uncle who served in the Marine Corps and two in the Army. One of those Army uncles was an ambulance driver in France, and his Victory Medal with its rainbow colored ribbon had a stepladder of battle clasps that listed his combat areas: Champagne-Marne, Aisne-Marne, St. Mihiel, Meuse-Argonne, and Defensive Sector. Of Hibernian ancestry and from New York City, he was a member of the "Fighting Irish" 69th Regiment of the celebrated Rainbow Division that landed in France in November of 1917.

Many of the songs from World War I carried over to WWII and still remain popular. These are good songs with catchy tunes and words that evoke vivid images. Although some could be complex in melody and harmony, most were basically simple and followed the standard format of "32-bar" songs from Tin Pan Alley.

Ukulele chords were introduced to sheet music following WWI as the ukulele soared into its first wave of popularity in the post-war Roaring 20s. But the instrument was also much in evidence during the war years right along with the parlor piano and wind-up Victrola.

Dick started playing the ukulele just about the time WWII was ending. His first instrument was a small soprano uke with cat gut strings which he played with an oval-shaped green felt pick that was soft and flexible. Few method books were available then, and Dick absorbed every one he could find. These books often included songs from WWI and they became part of Dick's standard repertoire -- and continue to be to this day.

From the soprano uke Dick graduated to the larger baritone made popular by radio star Arthur Godfrey. It went to college with Dick, later augmented by other instruments including the guitar and 4- and 5-string banjos. He continues to actively play and teach the uke and has written a number of books with arrangements for it and other instruments. He currently leads a Dixieland jazz band with which he has played tenor banjo for almost 50 years.

WE'RE IN THE ARMY NOW
(1917)
Ukulele tuning: gCEA

TELL TAYLOR & OLE OLSEN

ISHAM JONES

1.We're in the ar - my now, _____ we're not be-hind the plow, _____ we'll
nev - er get rich a - dig - gin' a ditch, we're in the ar - my now. _____ We're
in the ar - my now, _____ sup - pose you won - der how, _____ but
don't you fear, you'll soon be here, we're in the ar - my now. _____

2. We're in the army now, we're not behind the plow,
   *We're glad we're here that's why we cheer,
   We're in the army now.
   We're in the army now, suppose you wonder how,
   +We'll fight for right with all our might,
   We're in the army now.

3. *We'll do our share no matter where ...
   + Our U.S.A. needs us today ...

4. *The U-Boat war has gone too far ...
   +We'll do what's right, of course we'll fight ...

5. *We could sing all night, that wouldn't be right ...
   + We're losin' our pipes for the Stars and Stripes ...

PATRIOTIC WAR EDITION

At the time of World War I, the size of sheet music was often much larger than what we're used to today. A common size was 13-1/2" x 10-1/2." Announcements like the following began to appear:

> To co-operate with the Government and to conserve paper during the War, this song is issued in a smaller size than usual. Your co-operation will be very much appreciated.

LUCKY STRIKE GREEN

In a somewhat similar move during World War II, Lucky Strike cigarettes changed the main color of its packages from green to white. Allegedly it was to conserve the copper used in the green ink, but in reality it was an attempt to modernize the package's appearance. The slogan at the time of transition was:

"Lucky Strike Green has gone to war"

I DIDN'T RAISE MY BOY
TO BE A SOLDIER
(1915)

Ukulele tuning: gCEA

ALFRED BRYAN

AL PIANTADOSI

IF YOU WERE THE ONLY GIRL
(IN THE WORLD)
(1916)
Ukulele tuning: gCEA

CLIFFORD GREY

NAT D. AYER

"NEUTRAL" IS MY MIDDLE NAME

(1915)

Ukulele tuning: gCEA

Words & Music by
JACK FROST & JAMES WHITE

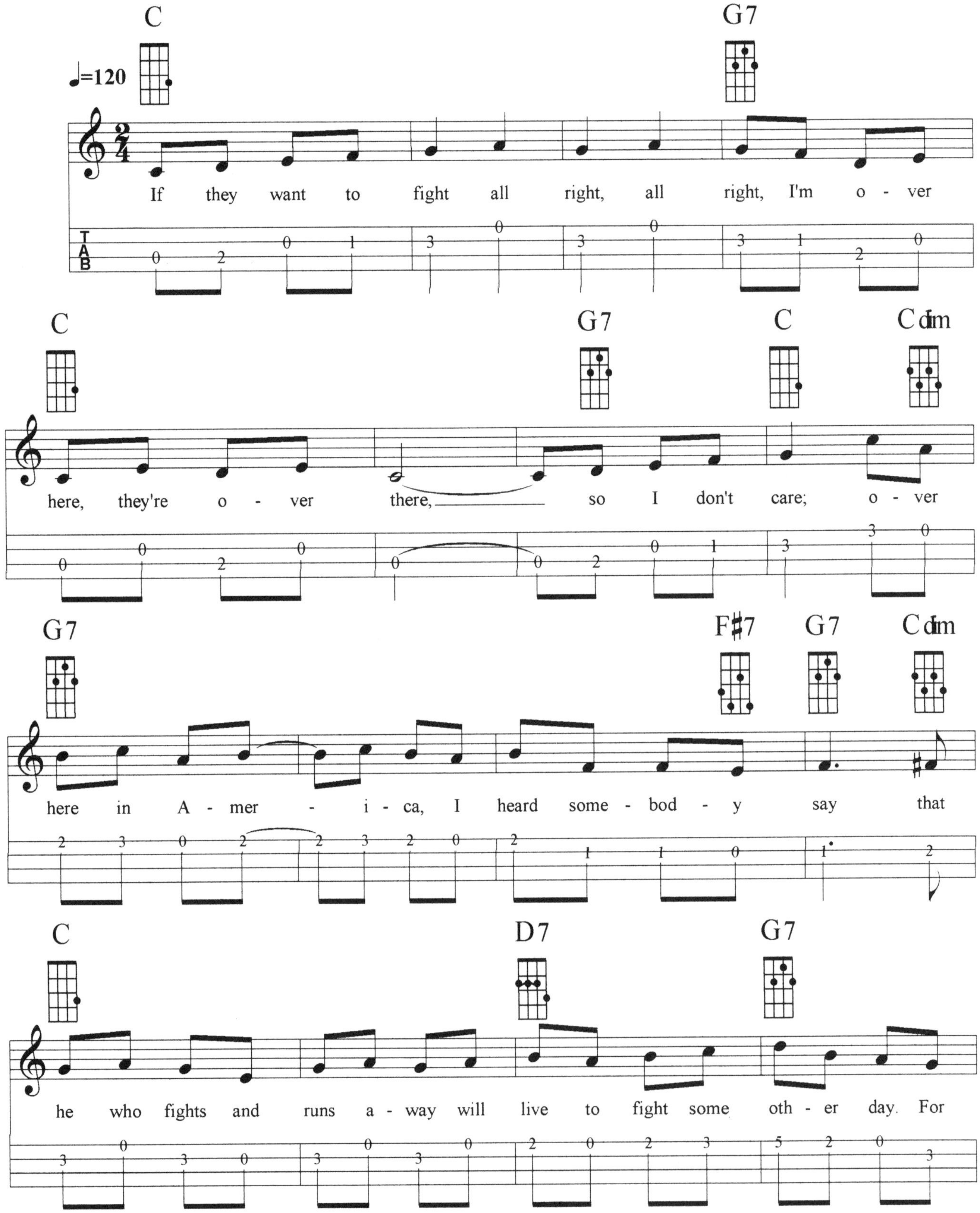

C
G7
♩=120
If they want to fight all right, all right, I'm o - ver
C
G7
C
C dim
here, they're o - ver there, so I don't care; o - ver
G7
F♯7
G7
C dim
here in A - mer - i - ca, I heard some - bod - y say that
C
D7
G7
he who fights and runs a - way will live to fight some oth - er day. For

NEUTRAL IS MY MIDDLE NAME

At the start of World War I most Americans favored the policy endorsed by President Wilson of strict neutrality. Public opinion began to sway with the sinking of the British passenger ship "Lusitania" and the loss of 128 American lives on board. Germany's program of unrestricted submarine warfare brought outrage, as did an intercepted message relayed from the German Empire to its ambassador in Mexico urging Mexico to join Germany if America entered the war. When the U.S. declared war on Germany in April 1917, most Americans were in full support.

I'm here and they're there, so what do I care,___ be - cause it's "Home, Sweet Home" just the same.___ While I'm as hap - py as can be be - hind the Sta - tue of Lib - er - ty, for "neu - tral" is my mid - dle name.___

GARRYOWEN

Ukulele tuning: gCEA

Traditional

An Irish "quickstep" long a favorite of military and marching bands. Its history precedes the Civil War and is currently the official march of the US 1st Cavalry Division. It is also the marching tune of New York's 69th Infantry Regiment, which is known both as the "Fighting 69th" and the "Fighting Irish."

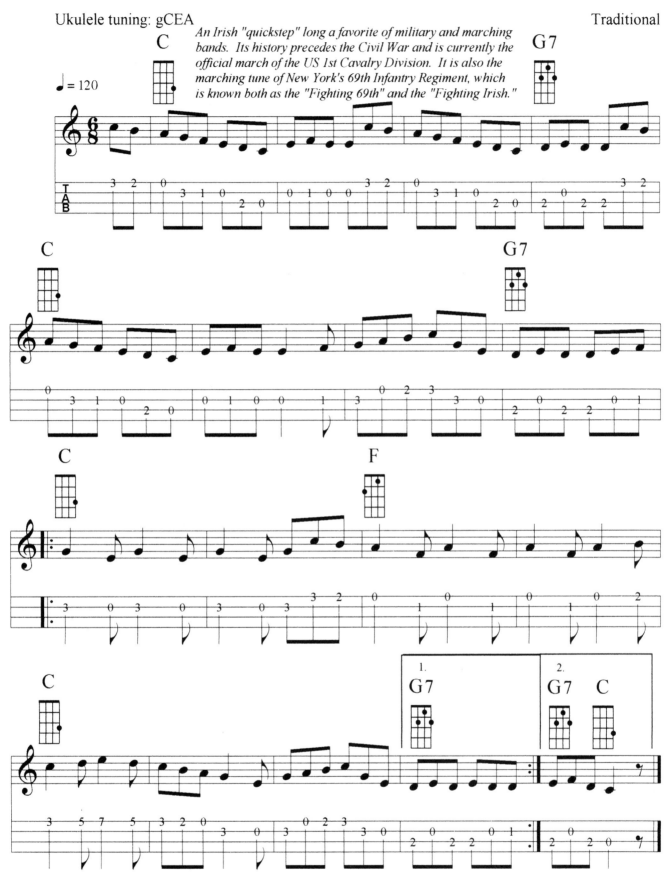

HOW 'YA GONNA KEEP 'EM DOWN ON THE FARM

(1918)

Ukulele tuning: gCEA

JOE YOUNG & SAM M. LEWIS

WALTER DONALDSON

How 'ya gon - na keep 'em down on the farm after they've seen Pa - ree? How 'ya gon - na keep 'em a - way from Broad - way,

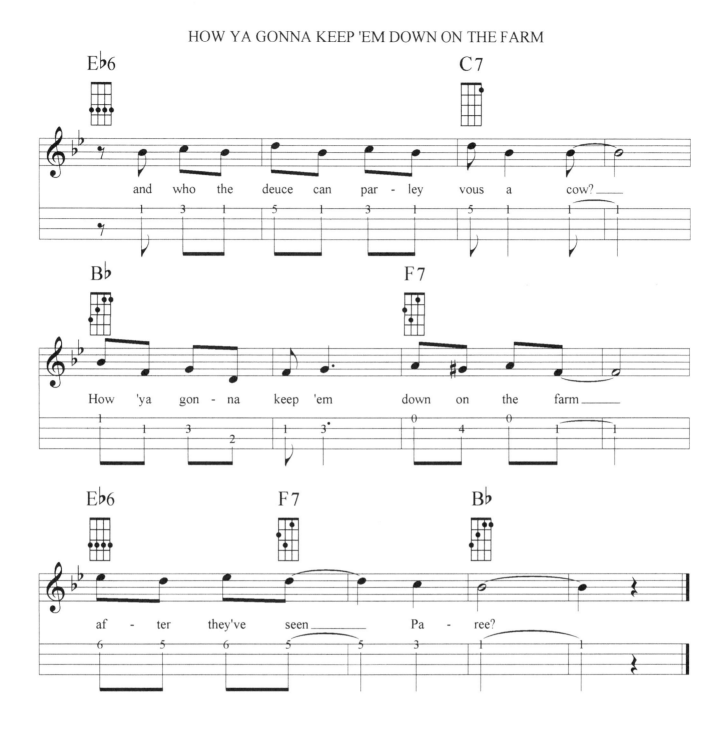

I'M ALWAYS CHASING RAINBOWS

(1917)

Ukulele tuning: gCEA

JOSEPH McCARTHY

HARRY CARROLL

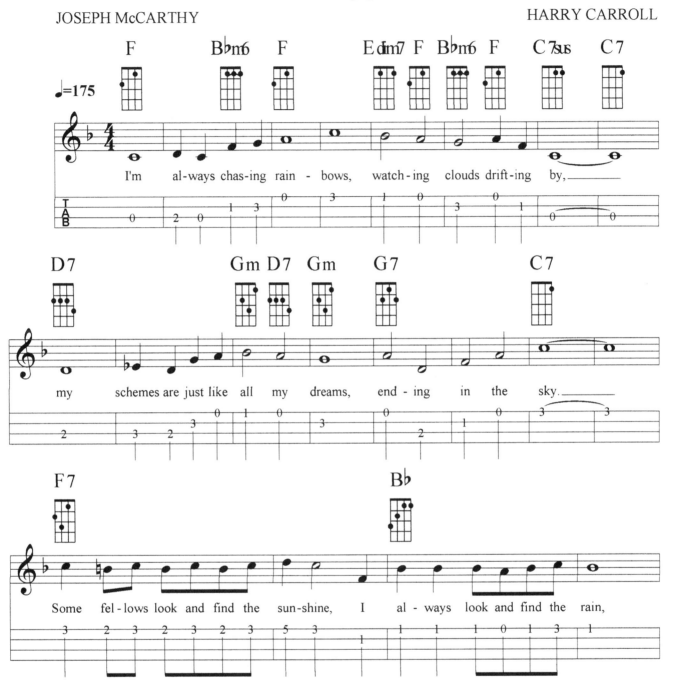

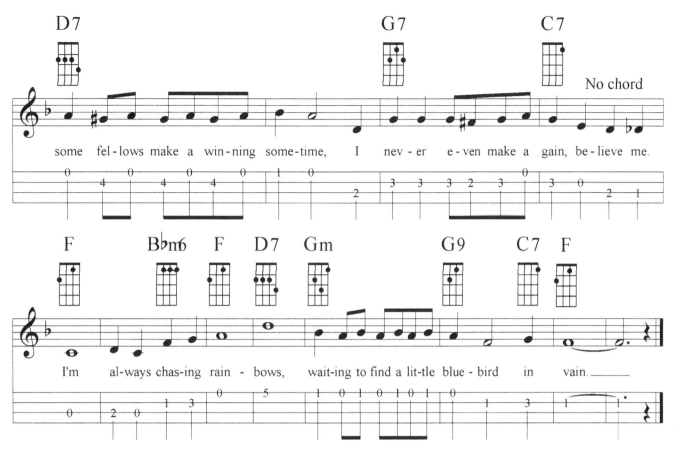

This popular song from the vaudeville stage was adapted from Frédéric Chopin's piano composition *Fantaisie-Impromtu in C-sharp minor*, which in turn shares similarities with Beethoven's *Moonlight Sonota*, also in the key of C-sharp minor.

BREAK THE NEWS TO MOTHER

(1897)

Ukulele tuning: gCEA

CHARLES K. HARRIS

GOOD-BYE, DOLLY GRAY
(1898)

Ukulele tuning: gCEA

WILL D. COBB   PAUL BARNES

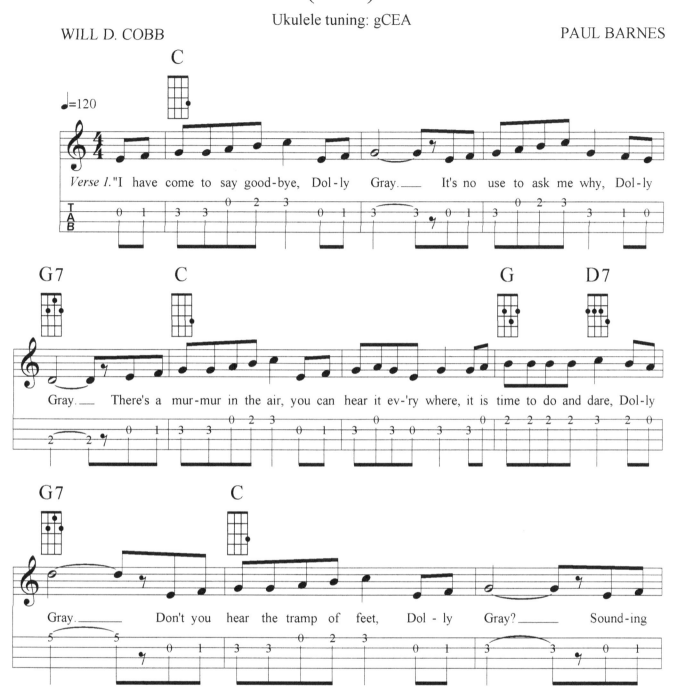

Verse 1. "I have come to say good-bye, Dol-ly Gray.___ It's no use to ask me why, Dol-ly Gray.___ There's a mur-mur in the air, you can hear it ev-'ry where, it is time to do and dare, Dol-ly Gray.___ Don't you hear the tramp of feet, Dol-ly Gray?___ Sound-ing

GOODBYE, DOLLY GRAY

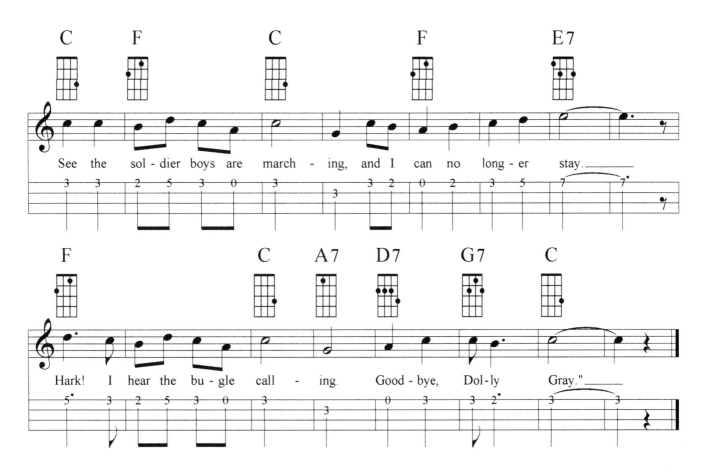

Verse 2. "Hear the rolling of the drums, Dolly Gray.
          Back from war the regiment comes, Dolly Gray.
          On your lovely face so fair, I can see a look of fear,
          For your soldier boy's not there, Dolly Gray.
          For the one you love so well, Dolly Gray,
          In the midst of battle fell, Dolly Gray,
          With his face toward the foe,
          As he died he murmured low,
          "I must say goodbye and go, Dolly Gray.""
          Chorus

Introduced in 1898 as a British music hall number, "Good-Bye, Dolly Gray" was sung that same year by American troops during the Spanish-American War. It gained popularity with British soldiers soon after at the time of the Boer War (1899 to 1902), and continued popular at the beginning of World War 1.

I WONDER WHO'S KISSING HER NOW
(1909)

WILL M. HOUGH
& FRANK R. ADAMS

Ukulele tuning: gCEA

JOSEPH E. HOWARD
& HAROLD ORLOB

IF I'M NOT AT THE ROLL-CALL

(1918)

Ukulele tuning: gCEA

GEORGE BOYDEN

'Twas just be - fore the bat - tle, boys, that day I'll ne'er for - get, _____ a

lad be - side me in the trench, as brave as I have met. _____ Tho'

death was near, he had no fear, 'twas ver - y plain to see, _____ for

just be - fore the bat - tle charge, he smil - ing - ly said to me: _____

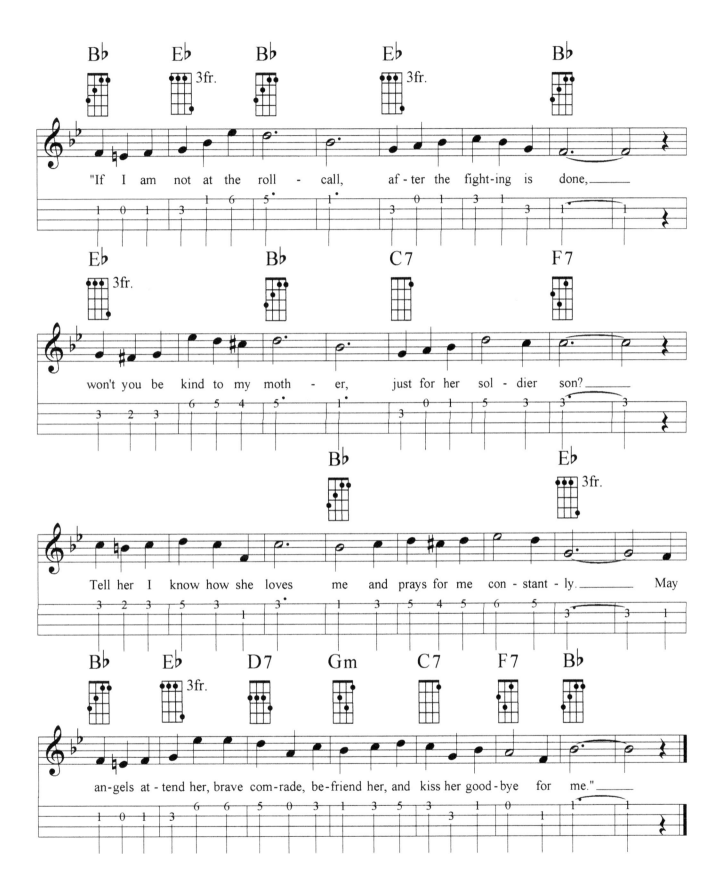

TILL WE MEET AGAIN

(1918)

Ukulele tuning: gCEA

RAYMOND B. EAGAN **RICHARD A. WHITING**

Smile the while you kiss me sad a - dieu,

when the clouds roll by I'll come to you.

Then the skies will seem more blue,

down in lov - ers lane, my dear - ie.

TILL WE MEET AGAIN

K-K-K-KATY

(1917)

Ukulele tuning: gCEA

GEOFFREY O'HARA

K - K - K - Ka - ty, beau - ti - ful Ka - ty, you're the

on - ly g - g - g - girl that I a - dore. When the m - m - m -

moon shines ov - er the cow shed, I'll be

wait - ing by the k - k - k - kitch - en door.

YANKEE BOY
(1919)

Ukulele tuning: gCEA

J. C. PALMER

Verse: 1. Yan-kee Boy, the day that you went a - way there were griev-ing hearts for you, ___ but you sang a song as you marched a - long 'neath the old Red, White and Blue. ___ Now the sweet re - frain of a Yan-kee strain comes from far a - cross the sea, ___ and a rous-ing cheer bids you wel - come here to the land of Lib - er - ty. ___

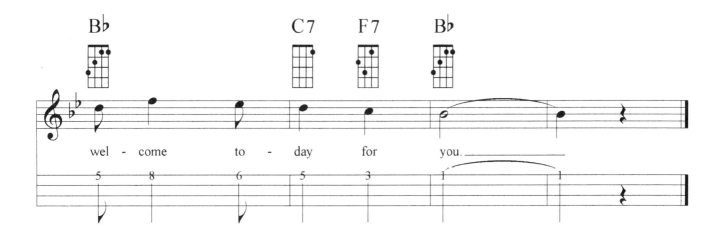

wel - come to - day for you. _____

Verse 2: We were proud of you and our Allies too
When you chased the Hun* away,
And our sailors true in their navy blue
Kept an open passage way.
Then the dawn of Peace caused the guns to cease
In that land across the sea,
And our Yankee Boy brings a world of joy
Coming home from Victory.
Chorus

*The Hun: a derogatory term for Germans. The medieval Hunnic Empire
was a belicose nomadic tribe led by "Attila, The Hun." Other
terms applied to Germans at the time of World War I were "Fritz,"
"Heinie,""Boche," and "Jerry" (more common in World War II.)
See also the song: "Hunting The Hun" included in this book.

OH! JOHNNY OH! JOHNNY OH!

(1917)

Ukulele tuning: gCEA

ED. ROSE

ABE OLMAN

OH! JOHNNY OH! JOHNNY OH!

Oh, Johnny! Oh, Johnny! why do you lag?
Oh, Johnny! Oh, Johnny! run to your flag!
Don't stay behind while others do all the fighting, start to ...
Oh, Johnny! Oh, Johnny! get right in line and help to crush the foe.
You're a big husky chap, Uncle Sam's in a scrap, you must
Go, Johnny! Go, Johnny! Go!

MY MELANCHOLY BABY

Ukulele tuning: gCEA

GEORGE A. NORTON

ERNIE BURNETT

There's an interesting story about Ernie Burnett (born Ernesto Marco Bernadetti), who wrote the music to "My Melancholy Baby." He had served in France during World War I with the 89th Division of the Allied Expeditionary Forces and was gassed in battle at Soissons. Because he had lost his memory as well as his dog-tags, there was no way his identity could be established. It happened that while Ernie was recuperating in the hospital, a victim of pulmonay illness and amnesia, a piano player who was entertaining the patients included "My Melancholy Baby" in his repertoire. On hearing the song, Ernie immediately recognized it and called out, "I wrote that song!" He had regained his memory!

Ernie went on to write more songs and stay active in the music business but he never again achieved the success of "My Melancholy Baby." Pulmonary problems continued to plague him and he moved to a "care cottage" in Saranac Lake, NY, married the proprietor, and died in the General Hospital there in 1959 at about the age of 74.

Saranac Lake in the Adirondack Mountains was well known for its clean air and sanatoria for pulmonary tuberculosis and respiratory ailments. Shortly after World War I the National Vaudeville Association established a care facility there for performers who were aging and ill. The sanatorium later became the Will Rogers Memorial Hospital named after the celebrated actor and humorist. Care was subsidized and made available to entertainers and support personnel from all areas of the theatrical world -- from movies, radio, TV, and the stage. Among the patients treated were Milton Berle, Phil Silvers, Jackie Gleason, and it is thought Al Jolson. For lack of funds the hospital was closed in 1974.

WHERE DO WE GO FROM HERE

(1917)

Ukulele tuning: gCEA

HOWARD JOHNSON &
PERCY WENRICH

Verse 1. Pad - dy Mack drove a hack up and down Broad - way,

Pat had one ex - press - ion, and he'd use it ev - 'ry day.

An - y time he'd grab a fare to take them for a ride,

Pad - dy jumped up on the seat, cracked his whip and cried:

WHERE DO WE GO FROM HERE

Verse 2. First of all, at the call, when the war began,
    Paddy signed up in the army as a fighting man.
    When the drills began they'd walk a hundred miles a day,
    Though the rest got tired, Paddy always used to say:
    CHORUS

I'VE GOT MY CAPTAIN
WORKING FOR ME NOW

(1919)

Ukulele tuning: gCEA

IRVING BERLIN

Lyrics:
I've got the guy ___ who used to be my Cap-tain work-ing ___ for me, ___

he want-ed work ___ so I made him a clerk ___ in my fa-ther's fac-to-ry. ___ And bye and

bye ___ I'm gon-na have him wrapped in work up to his brow. ___ I make him

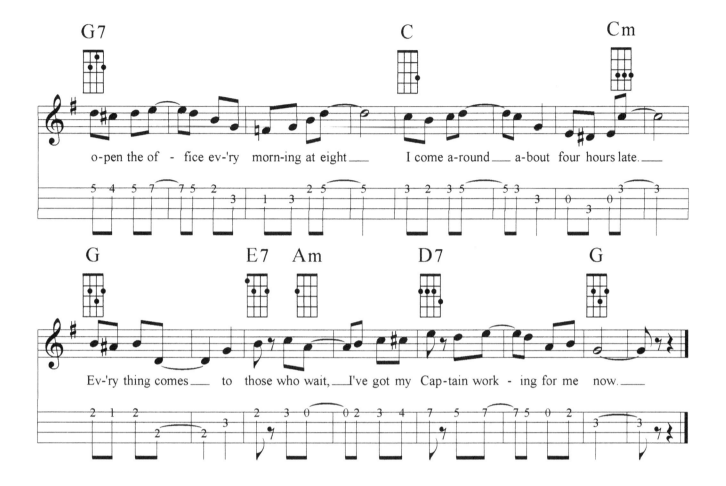

o-pen the of - fice ev-'ry morn-ing at eight___ I come a-round___ a-bout four hours late.___

Ev-'ry thing comes___ to those who wait,___I've got my Cap-tain work - ing for me now.___

WOULD YOU RATHER BE A COLONEL
WITH AN EAGLE ON YOUR SHOULDER
(1919)

Ukulele tuning: gCEA

ARCHIE GOTTLER

"I'd rath - er be a pri - vate than a colonel in the ar - my, a

pri - vate has more fun when his day's work is done, and

when he goes on hikes, in ev - 'ry town he strikes,

girls dis - cov - er him, and just smoth - er him with things he likes. But girl - ies

OH! HOW I HATE TO GET UP IN THE MORNING
(1918)

Ukulele tuning: gCEA

IRVING BERLIN

SMILES

(1917)

J. WILL CALLAHAN

LEE S. ROBERTS

Smiles was a sentimental favorite all through the war, becoming a standard of World War 1.
Lee Roberts reportedly wrote the tune on the back of a cigarette package

HAIL! HAIL! THE GANG'S ALL HERE!

(1917)

Ukulele tuning: gCEA

D.A. ESROM

THEODORE MORE
(Chorus from ARTHUR SULLIVAN)

HAIL! HAIL! THE GANG'S ALL HERE!

G

Recognize the melody of the chorus? It's a takeoff from Gilbert & Sullivan's comic opera *Pirates of Penzance* and was inspired by Giuseppe Verdi's *Anvil Chorus* from the opera *Il Trovatore*.

Verse 2. We love one another, we do, we do, we do,
With brotherly love, and it's true, it's true, it's true,
One for all, the big and small, it's always me for you;
No matter the weather when we get together,
We drink a toast or two.
CHORUS

GOODBYE BROADWAY, HELLO FRANCE
(1917)

Ukulele tuning: gCEA

C. FRANCIS REISNER & BENNY DAVIS

BILLY BASKETTE

Good - bye Broad - way, hel - lo France, ___

we're ten mil - lion strong. ___

Good - bye sweet - hearts, wives and moth - ers,

it won't take us long. ___

GOODBYE BROADWAY, HELLO FRANCE

Indeed, as these lyrics remind us, America had a debt to square with France. During the American Revolution, France proved to be a great ally against the British, providing money in the form of loans and grants, along with arms, naval forces and combat troops. When Gen. Pershing arrived in France in 1917, he visited the tomb of the Marquis de Lafayette who had served as a general under George Washington. It was there that the famous words were spoken, "Lafayette, we are here!"

MADEMOISELLE FROM ARMENTIÈRES

(Circa 1914)

Ukulele tuning: gCEA

Traditional melody

OH! FRENCHY
(1918)
Ukulele tuning: gCEA

SAM EHRLICH

CON CONRAD

Oh! French - y,_____ Oh! French - y, French - y,_____ al - tho' your

lan - guage is so new to me. When you

say, "Oui, oui, la, la"_____

"We," means you and me, la, la._____ Oh!

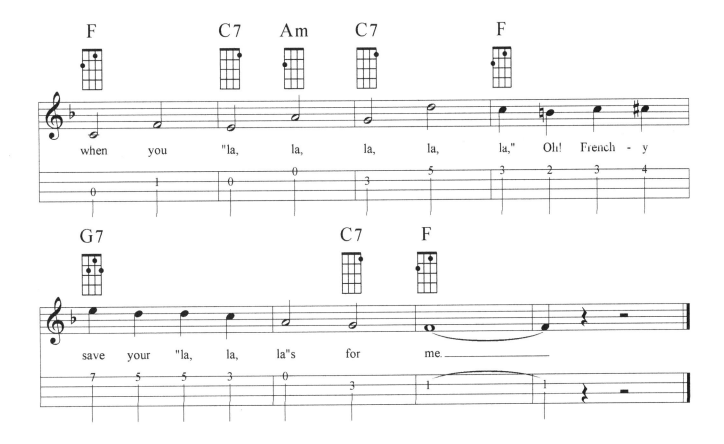

when you "la, la, la, la, la," Oh! French - y

save your "la, la, la"s for me._____

Soldiers stationed in France during World War I weren't the only ones to form romantic attachments. American women serving overseas as nuses, bilingual telephone operators, and stenographers had their romances too -- with French men. For a screwball post-WWII comedy with a reversal of roles, check out the 1949 film "I Was A Male War Bride" starring Cary Grant and Ann Sheridan.

OUI, OUI, MARIE

(1918)

ALFRED BRYAN and
JOE McCARTHY

Ukulele tuning: gCEA

FRED FISHER

OUI, OUI, MARIE

DON'T CRY, FRENCHY, DON'T CRY

(1919)

Ukulele tuning: gCEA

SAM M. LEWIS & JOE YOUNG

WALTER DONALDSON

"Don't cry, French-y, don't cry, when you kiss me good-bye, I will al-ways keep the Fleur-de-lis, dear, you gave to me, dear, so dry you eye.

DON'T CRY, FRENCHY, DON'T CRY

Just as in "Don't Cry, Frenchy. Don't Cry," wartime romances were not uncommon.
Soldiers on leave or stationed in a foreign country often formed relationships that
sometimes resulted in marraiage. Following WWI there were many war brides who
emigrated from their native homes to rejoin husbands for a new life in a new land.

LA MARSEILLAISE
French National Anthem
(1792)

Ukulele tuning: gCEA

JEAN-CLAUDE ROUGET DE LISLE

LA MARSEILLAISE

ENGLISH TRANSLATION

Arise, children of the homeland, the day of glory has arrived!
Against us tyranny, the bloody banner is raised, the bloody banner is raised.
Do you hear in the countryside the roar of those ferocious soldiers?
They're coming right into your arms to cut the throats of your sons and women.
To arms, citizens, form your battalions. Let's march, let's march!
Let an impure blood water our furrows.

DARDANELLA
(1919)
Ukulele tuning: gCEA

FRED FISHER

FELIX BERNARD &
JOHNNY S. BLACK

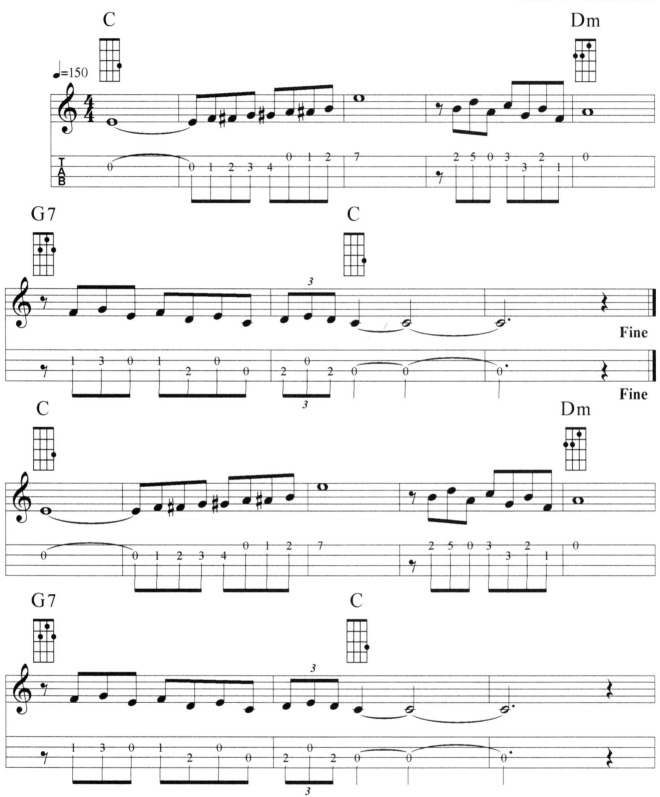

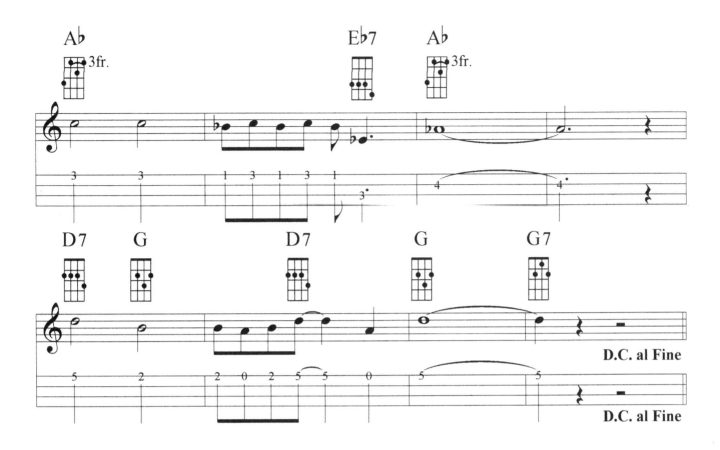

In October of 1914, Turkey (then known as the Ottoman Empire) enterered the war on the side of Germany and Austria-Hungary. Winston Churchill who was the First Lord of the British Admiralty decided to attack Turkey and seize control of the Dardanelles Strait. This would open a supply route from the Aegean Sea to Russian ports on the Black Seas and create a diversion of Turkish troops from the Eastern Front. It was also hoped that a victory would cause Bulgaria to join the Allies. The sea battle proved disasterous and land action on the Gallipoli Peninsula, which was bordered on one side by the Dardanelles, was also a defeat for Allied troops. Bulgaria went over to the Central Powers, and Churchill resigned his government post, although he later resumed that position during World War II and then, of course, became Prime Minister.

HELLO, CENTRAL! GIVE ME NO MAN'S LAND
(1918)

SAM M. LEWIS
& JOE YOUNG

Ukulele tuning: gCEA

JEAN SCHWARTZ

HELLO, CENTRAL! GIVE ME NO MAN'S LAND

THERE'S A LONG, LONG TRAIL

Ukulele tuning: gCEA

STODDARD KING

ALONZO "ZO" ELLIOTT

OVER THERE

(1917)

Ukulele tuning: gCEA

GEORGE M. COHAN

Verse 2. Johnnie get your gun, get your gun, get your gun,
Johnnie show the Hun you're a son-of-a-gun,
Hoist the flag and let her fly,
Like true heroes, do or die.
Pack your little kit, show your grit, do your bit,
Soldiers to the ranks from the towns and the tanks,
Make your mother proud of you,
And to liberty be true.
CHORUS

*George M. Cohan composed this song on April 6, 1917, the very morning the
United States declared war on Germany. So popular was the song that by the
end of the war over two million copies had been sold. In 1936 Cohan was
awarded the Congressional Gold medal for this and other patriotic songs he
had written.*

THE ROSE OF NO MAN'S LAND
(1918)

Ukulele tuning: gCEA

JACK CADDIGAN   JAMES A. BRENNAN

I've seen some beau-ti-ful flow - ers, grow in life's gar-den fair,

I've spent some won-der-ful hours___ lost in their fra-grance rare.

But I have found an-oth - er, won-drous be-yond com - pare.___ There's a

THE WORLD IS WAITING FOR THE SUNRISE
(1919)
Ukulele tuning: gCEA

EUGENE LOCKHART

ERNEST SEITZ

THE FIGHTING SIXTY-NINTH

Ukulele tuning: gCEA

ANNA L. HAMILTON

THE FIGHTING SIXTY-NINTH

*The 69th Infantry Regiment of the New York National Guard traces
its history back to the Civil War. It was sent to France in October of
1917 and saw combat in the battles of Champagne, Château-Thierry,
St. Mihel and the Meuse-Argonne. Its ranks were composed mostly of
New Yorkers, many of whom were of Irish heritage, giving rise to its
other nickname, "The Fighting Irish." It was this title that was later
adopted by the football team of the University of Notre Dame.*

THE FIGHTING SIXTY-NINTH

Notable among the ranks of the "Fighting 69th" was the poet Joyce Kilmer who wrote the well-known poem
"Trees." He was killed in the battle of Château-Thierry in July of 1918. Also celebrated is Father Francis Duffy,
a non-combatant, who nonetheless earned the title of "The Fighting Chaplin" owing to his many acts of heroism
on the front lines. A statue of him stands in Duffy Square in the Times Square area of New York City between 45th
and 47th Streets, Broadway and 7th Avenue. The Square is also shared by another statue, that of George M Cohan.

DOWN IN THE U-17

(1915)

Ukulele tuning: gCEA

ROGER LEWIS

ERNIE ERDMAN

The term U-boat comes from the German "unterseeboot" literally "under sea boat."

HUNTING THE HUN

(1918)

Ukulele tuning: g-CEA

HOWARD E. ROGERS

ARCHIE GOTTLER

Verses: 1.O-ver in France there's a game that's played by all the sol-dier boys in each bri-gade.

2.I met a sol - dier and he told me, it's just the lat-est thing a-cross the sea.

It's called Hunt -ing the Hun. This is how it is done._____ First you

It's a game that is new, they're all do - ing it too._____

Chorus: go get a gun, then you look for a Hun, then you start on a run for the son of a gun,

Hun: A disparaging term applied initially by the British to mock German soldiers. The Huns were a fierce nomadic Mongolian people under Atilla who invaded central and eastern Europe around 450 A.D. Kaiser Wilhelm II linked the might of the Huns to his forces in 1900 as they were leaving for China during the Boxer Rebellion.

The helmets worn by German troops until 1916 were reminiscent of those worn by the Huns. Called "Pickelhauben" (literally *pick bonnets*) they were made of hardened boiled leather with a metal spike on the top. The shape was changed to the familiar style of World War II and the leather replaced by steel. The helmet was then known as a "Stahlhelm."

THE CAISSONS GO ROLLING ALONG

(1908)

Ukulele tuning: gCEA

ROBERT M. DANFORD
& WILLIAM BRYDEN

EDMUND L. GRUBER

Verse 2. To the front, day and night,
Where the doughboys dig and fight,
And those caissons go rolling along.
Our barrage will be there,
Fired on the rocket's flare,
While those caissons go rolling along.
CHORUS

AVALON

(1920)

AL JOLSON
B. G. DeSILVA

Ukulele tuning: gCEA

VINCENT ROSE

I found my love in Av - a - lon ____ be -
side ____ the bay, ____ I left my love in
Av - a - lon, ____ and sail'd ____ a - way. ____ I
dream of her and Av - a - lon ____ from dusk ____ till

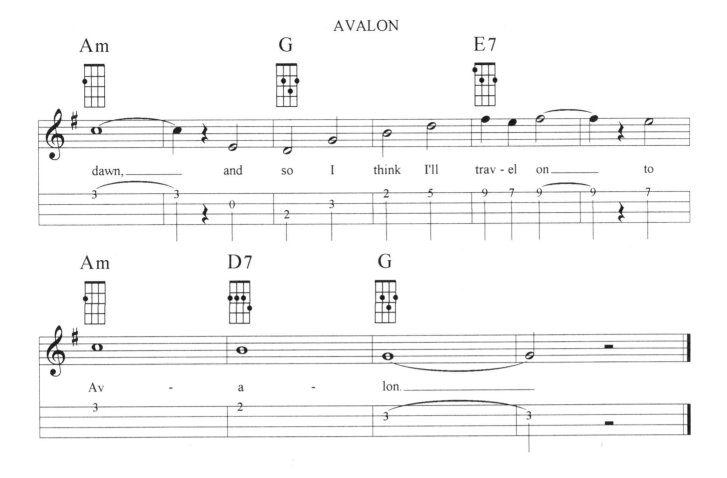

Am   **G**   **E7**

dawn,   and   so   I   think   I'll   trav - el   on   to

Am   **D7**   **G**

Av - a - lon.

HIS MASTER'S VOICE
Many of the songs in this collection were transcribed from
early 78rpm recordings put out by the Victor Talking Machine
Company on a VICTOR label. The logo on each black & gold
label displayed a fox terrier dog (named Nipper) listening and
looking into the speaker bell of a wind-up cylinder phonograph.
Below the image of the phonograph and Nipper were the words
"His master's voice."

GOOD NIGHT, GERMANY
(If He Can Fight Like He Can Love)

Ukulele tuning: gCEA

GRANT CLARKE &
HOWARD E. ROGERS

GEORGE W. MEYER

SILENT NIGHT
(1818)

JOSEPH MOHR   Ukulele tuning: gCEA   FRANZ GRUBER

Si - lent night, ho - ly night, all is calm, all is bright,
Stil - le Nacht, hei - li - ge Nacht! Al - les schläft, ein - sam wacht,

'round yon Vir - gin moth - er and Child, ho - ly In - fant so ten - der and mild,
Nur das trau - te hock - hei - li - ge Paar, Hol - der Kna - be im lok - ki - gen Haar,

sleep in heav - en - ly peace,___ sleep___ in heav - en - ly peace.___
Schlaf in himm - li - scher Ruh,___ Schlaf ___ in himm - li - scher Ruh!___

CHRISTMAS TRUCE
(Weihnachtfreiden)

It was Christmas Eve 1914, just a few months after the start of World War I, when in some sections of the Western Front the terrible fighting was interrupted by one of the most bizarre occurences of the war. A silence settled in from the firing of guns and the exploding bombs. Gradually voices were heard on both sides of No Man's Land, first timid then growing louder, calling out Christmas greetings across the trenches, "Frohe Weihnachten! Happy Christmas! Joyeux Noël!" It is said to have started with the German troops as they sang and put up Christmas trees, some with lighted candles. The holiday spirit was soon caught by the British and the French. Greetings and carols were exchanged, troops ventured out of the trenches, hands were shaken, food and tobacco shared, souvenirs of buttons and hats were traded. Informal games of soccer broke out with participants playing from both sides. The unofficial lull also afforded an opportunity for the more serious business of burial ceremonies, yet the feeling of celebration lasted through Christmas Day and in some sections on to New Year's Day.

RULE BRITANNIA
(1740)

Words from a poem by
JAMES THOMSON

Ukulele tuning: gCEA

THOMAS AUGUSTINE ARNE

G   C   D 7

♩=80

Rule   Bri - tan - nia,   Bri - tan - nia rules   the waves,

G   D 7 G

Bri - tons   nev - er, nev - er, nev - er   shall   be   slaves.

GOD SAVE THE KING
British National Anthem
(1745)

Ukulele tuning: gCEA

Anonymous

G   D 7   G   C   G   D 7   G

♩=120

God save our   gra - cious King! Long live our   no - ble King! God save the   King!

GOD SAVE THE KING

George V (1865-1936) reigned as king of England from 1910 to 1936. In 1917 the family name was changed to Windsor from the German sounding Saxe-Coburg-Gotha. On several occasions George and his wife Queen Mary visited the Western Front. He was seriously injured when his horse rolled over on him breaking his pelvis, an accident from which he never fully recovered.

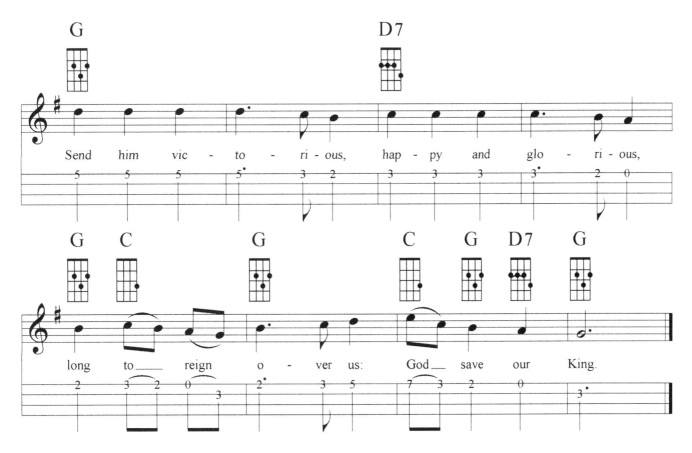

Send him vic - to - ri - ous, hap - py and glo - ri - ous,

long to reign o - ver us: God save our King.

IT'S A LONG WAY TO TIPPERARY

Ukulele tuning: gCEA

JACK JUDGE &
HARRY WILLIAMS

BACK IN THE U.S.A.
(1917)
Ukulele tuning: gCEA

BYFORD F. INMAN

EUGENE E. NOEL

Last night I thought of that won-der-ful girl I left in the U. S. A,

heard her wist-ful sigh as I said good - bye on that e - vent-ful part-ing day. I

fan - cied I held her in my arms, ca - ressed her ten - der cheek, she

raised her tear - ful eyes to mine, I e - ven heard her speak:___ You're goin' to

YOU'RE A GRAND OLD FLAG
(1906)

Ukulele tuning: gCEA

GEORGE M. COHAN

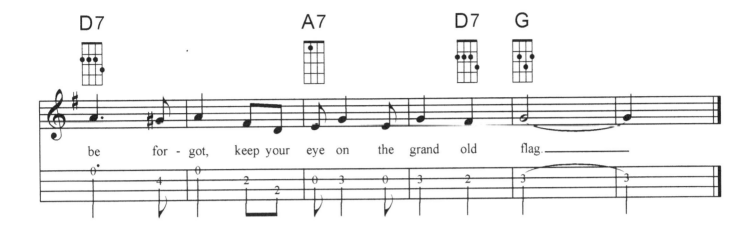

be   for - got,   keep your   eye   on   the   grand   old   flag.

THERE'S A SERVICE FLAG
FLYING AT OUR HOUSE

Ukulele tuning: gCEA

THOMAS P. HOIER
BERNIE GROSSMAN

A. W. BROWN

THERE'S A SERVICE FLAG FLYING AT OUR HOUSE

Just as today, service flags were flown during World War I. The flag has not changed and is the same now as it was then: a red field on which is inset a white rectangle with one or more blue stars indicating the number of family members in active military service.

TAPS

Although much is uncertain as to the origin of this haunting tune, the name, and the lyrics, it apparently traces back to the Civil War. It was offically adopted by the Army in 1874 and regularly used for military funerals after 1891. A chilling effect is heard when two trumpets play, one echoing the other, phrase by phrase.

Fading light	Thanks and praise	Then good night,
Dims the sight,	For our days	Peaceful night,
And a star	'Neath the sun,	Till the light
Gems the sky	'Neath the stars,	Of the dawn
Glowing bright.	'Neath the sky.	Shineth bright.
From afar	As we go	God is night,
Drawing nigh	This we know,	Do not fear,
Falls the night.	God is nigh.	Friend, good night.

Heard around the world every day. The most famous 3 notes in musical history.